GREAT ENGLISH POETS

GREAT ENGLISH POETS

John Donne

Edited and with an introduction
by Peter Porter

 Clarkson N. Potter, Inc./Publishers NEW YORK
DISTRIBUTED BY CROWN PUBLISHERS, INC.

Selection and Introduction copyright © 1988 by Peter Porter

Published in the United States by Clarkson N. Potter, Inc.,
225 Park Avenue South, New York, New York 10003
and represented in Canada by the Canadian MANDA Group.
Published in Great Britain by Aurum Press Ltd.,
33 Museum Street, London WC1A 1LD, England.

CLARKSON N. POTTER, POTTER, THE GREAT POETS,
and colophon are trademarks of Clarkson N. Potter, Inc.

Picture research by Juliet Brightmore

Manufactured in Hong Kong

Library of Congress Cataloging-in-Publication Data

Donne, John, 1572–1631.
    [Poems. Selections]
    John Donne/edited and with an introduction by Peter Porter.
    p. cm. — (Great English poets)

    I. Porter, Peter.   II. Title.   III. Series.

PR2246.P67   1988   88–17751   821'.3—dc19
ISBN 0–517–57011–4

    10 9 8 7 6 5 4 3 2 1

First Edition

CONTENTS

INTRODUCTION

John Donne enjoys the reputation of being one of the most passionate love poets in literature, but there are so many other observations which have to be made about him – as poet, courtier, lover, divine, husband and friend – that his whole life may be scanned as a divided pilgrimage. His career goes one way and his writing another. The one factor common to both is his passion, almost always pitched at the very edge of excess. The youthful lover and the sonorous Dean of St Paul's are both wooers. In his spirited twenties Donne wooed women: once ordained, he pursued God just as ardently. In between lay much bitter experience and real grief.

The most personal of the Holy Sonnets, 'Since she whom I loved' (p. 56), is a lament for his wife, Ann, dead at the age of thirty-three. The desolation and regret are sincere, but the poem turns at the end to God. Donne's marriage was the most profound event of his life, a source of reality in an imagination feverish and fantastical. Yet it is hard not to feel that it was his wife who paid the higher price for the triumphs of Donne's great days as preacher and theologian. She bore him eleven children and shared with him the disappointments of his early career. Great poet that he was, his personality was suffused with egotism, and it is this very egotism, tumbling from his pen with unmatched virtuosity, which startles us across four centuries.

Donne's family on his mother's side were recusants, and he suffered throughout his life from a certain schizophrenia in religion. His loyalty and his intellect supported the Reformed Church of England, but his

Roman Catholic sympathies went deep. He had a powerful reason for taking the Anglican side in the religious controversies of the Counter Reformation: that was the only way to get preferment, and he was highly ambitious. Since he was born in 1572, the monarch he had to please was the secretive and suspicious King James I. But Donne ruined his chances of advancement by his clandestine marriage at the end of the century, and for the first decade of James's reign he was forced to linger far from Court, at Mitcham in Surrey. During this time he travelled to Europe on several ambassadorial ventures. As a young man he had been on unofficial raiding expeditions to Spain, and he now became well acquainted with France, Germany and the Low Countries. His friend Thomas Coryate (see p. 37) was a well-known traveller.

It was during this period of eclipse that Donne wrote his most impassioned religious poetry, in particular the Holy Sonnets. These superbly wrought products of his guilt are really poems in search of faith, not statements of belief. They are the finest examples of baroque in English literature, the equivalent in words of Bernini's architecture and sculpture.

In a vain attempt to restore himself to favour, Donne undertook the composing of polemical pamphlets against the King's ecclesiastical enemies. But eventually he was forced to abandon his ambitions of worldly success and accept the King's determination that his vocation should be in the Church. Once he was ordained, at the age of forty-three, poetry began to desert him.

As Dean of St Paul's, Donne became famous for his

baroque sermons. But as a young student at the Inns of Court he had already earned a reputation as a fashionable poet. Although his poems were not published until after his death, so many copies of them survive that we know how widely circulated they were. The school of poetry we call Metaphysical owes its whole existence to his influence. George Herbert, Henry Vaughan, Richard Crashaw and a host of lesser writers are 'School of Donne'. He was, perhaps, the greatest poetic innovator in the English language. This is the more remarkable when one remembers that the majority of his songs and lyrics were written in his extreme youth, in the years 1591 to 1594. This is the Donne of the fantastical portrait (see frontispiece) – extravagantly dressed, with red sensual lips, the man described by a friend as 'very neat, a great visiter of ladies'. Donne trained in the law, and his sensuous love poems are paradoxically also cases argued with legal precision and wit. However extreme the conceits and comparisons, his writing is always true to the naturalistic surface of life. Nothing can stale these audacious poems. They are exaggerations we know to be more true than any measured description could ever be.

In this selection, I have endeavoured to represent the two strands of Donne's poetry – the pleas of the passionate lover, and the cries of the penitent believer. A few of his more scurrilous humorous burlesques are also included. There is little stylistic difference among his several genres. Love and death are always present. The youthful melancholic who poses for his portrait in dandified dress is also the dying churchman who has himself painted in his winding sheet. Donne is never moderate; instead, he lives always on the high ground.

Song

Go, and catch a falling star,
   Get with child a mandrake root,
Tell me, where all past years are,
   Or who cleft the Devil's foot,
Teach me to hear mermaids singing,
   Or to keep off envy's stinging,
         And find
         What wind
Serves to advance an honest mind.

If thou be'est born to strange sights,
   Things invisible to see,
Ride ten thousand days and nights,
   Till age snow white hairs on thee,
Thou, when thou return'st, wilt tell me
All strange wonders that befell thee,
         And swear
         No where
Lives a women true, and fair.

If thou find'st one, let me know,
   Such a pilgrimage were sweet,
Yet do not, I would not go,
   Though at next door we might meet,
Though she were true, when you met her,
And last, till you write your letter,
         Yet she
         Will be
False, ere I come, to two, or three.

The Good Morrow

I wonder by my troth, what thou, and I
    Did, till we loved? were we not weaned till
       then,
But sucked on country pleasures, childishly?
    Or snorted we in the seven sleepers' den?
'Twas so; but this, all pleasures fancies be.
If ever any beauty I did see,
Which I desired, and got, 'twas but a dream of
    thee.

And now good morrow to our waking souls,
    Which watch not one another out of fear;
For love, all love of other sights controls,
    And makes one little room, an every where.
Let sea-discoverers to new worlds have gone,
Let maps to others, worlds on worlds have
    shown,
Let us possess one world, each hath one, and is
    one.

My face in thine eye, thine in mine appears,
    And true plain hearts do in the faces rest,
Where can we find two better hemispheres
    Without sharp north, without declining west?
What ever dies, was not mixed equally;
If our two loves be one, or, thou and I
Love so alike, that none do slacken, none can die.

The Bait

Come live with me, and be my love,
And we will some new pleasures prove
Of golden sands, and crystal brooks,
With silken lines, and silver hooks.

There will the river whispering run
Warmed by thy eyes, more than the sun.
And there th'enamoured fish will stay,
Begging themselves they may betray.

When thou wilt swim in that live bath,
Each fish, which every channel hath,
Will amorously to thee swim,
Gladder to catch thee, than thou him.

If thou, to be so seen, be'st loth,
By sun, or moon, thou darkenest both,
And if myself have leave to see,
I need not their light, having thee.

Let others freeze with angling reeds,
And cut their legs, with shells and weeds,
Or treacherously poor fish beset,
With strangling snare, or windowy net:

Let coarse bold hands, from slimy nest
The bedded fish in banks out-wrest,
Or curious traitors, sleavesilk flies
Bewitch poor fishes' wandering eyes.

For thee, thou need'st no such deceit,
For thou thyself art thine own bait,
That fish, that is not catched thereby,
Alas, is wiser far than I.

A Lecture upon the Shadow

Stand still, and I will read to thee
A lecture, love, in love's philosophy.
    These three hours that we have spent,
    Walking here, two shadows went
Along with us, which we ourselves produced;
But, now the sun is just above our head,
    We do those shadows tread;
    And to brave clearness all things are reduced.
  So whilst our infant loves did grow,
Disguises did, and shadows, flow,
From us, and our care; but, now 'tis not so.

That love hath not attained the high'st degree,
Which is still diligent lest others see.

Except our loves at this noon stay,
We shall new shadows make the other way.
    As the first were made to blind
    Others; these which come behind
Will work upon ourselves, and blind our eyes.
If our loves faint, and westwardly decline;
    To me thou, falsely, thine,
    And I to thee mine actions shall disguise.
  The morning shadows wear away,
But these grow longer all the day,
But oh, love's day is short, if love decay.

Love is a growing, or full constant light;
And his first minute, after noon, is night.

The Sun Rising

Busy old fool, unruly sun,
Why dost thou thus,
Through windows, and through curtains call on us?
Must to thy motions lovers' seasons run?
Saucy pedantic wretch, go chide
Late school-boys, and sour prentices,
Go tell court-huntsmen, that the King will ride,
Call country ants to harvest offices;
Love, all alike, no season knows, nor clime,
Nor hours, days, months, which are the rags of time.

Thy beams, so reverend, and strong
Why shouldst thou think?
I could eclipse and cloud them with a wink,
But that I would not lose her sight so long:
If her eyes have not blinded thine,
Look, and tomorrow late, tell me,
Whether both th'Indias of spice and mine
Be where thou left'st them, or lie here with me.
Ask for those kings whom thou saw'st yesterday,
And thou shalt hear, All here in one bed lay.

She'is all states, and all princes, I,
Nothing else is.
Princes do but play us; compared to this,
All honour's mimic; all wealth alchemy.
Thou sun art half as happy as we,
In that the world's contracted thus;

Thine age asks ease, and since thy duties be
To warm the world, that's done in warming us.
Shine here to us, and thou art everywhere;
This bed thy centre is, these walls, thy sphere.

Break of Day

'Tis true, 'tis day, what though it be?
O wilt thou therefore rise from me?
Why should we rise, because 'tis light?
Did we lie down, because 'twas night?
Love which in spite of darkness brought us hither,
Should in despite of light keep us together.

Light hath no tongue, but is all eye;
If it could speak as well as spy,
This were the worst, that it could say,
That being well, I fain would stay,
And that I loved my heart and honour so,
That I would not from him, that had them, go.

Must business thee from hence remove?
Oh, that's the worst disease of love,
The poor, the foul, the false, love can
Admit but not the busied man.
He which hath business, and makes love, doth do
Such wrong, as when a married man doth woo.

The Anniversary

All kings, and all their favourites,
  All glory of honours, beauties, wits,
The sun itself, which makes times, as they pass,
Is elder by a year, now, than it was
When thou and I first one another saw:
All other things, to their destruction draw,
  Only our love hath no decay;
This, no tomorrow hath, nor yesterday,
Running it never runs from us away,
But truly keeps his first, last, everlasting day.

  Two graves must hide thine and my corse,
  If one might, death were no divorce,
Alas, as well as other princes, we,
(Who prince enough in one another be,)
Must leave at last in death, these eyes, and ears,
Oft fed with true oaths, and with sweet salt tears;
  But souls where nothing dwells but love
(All other thoughts being inmates) then shall
      prove
This, or a love increased there above,
When bodies to their graves, souls from their
      graves remove.

  And then we shall be throughly blessed,
  But we no more, than all the rest.
Here upon earth, we are kings, and none but we
Can be such kings, nor of such subjects be;

Who is so safe as we? where none can do
Treason to us, except one of us two.
    True and false fears let us refrain,
Let us love nobly, and live, and add again
Years and years unto years, till we attain
To write threescore, this is the second of our reign.

Woman's Constancy

Now thou hast loved me one whole day,
Tomorrow when thou leav'st, what wilt thou say?
Wilt thou then antedate some new made vow?
                Or say that now
We are not just those persons, which we were?
Or, that oaths made in reverential fear
Of Love, and his wrath, any may forswear?
Or, as true deaths, true marriages untie,
So lovers' contracts, images of those,
Bind but till sleep, death's image, them unloose?
                Or, your own end to justify,
For having purposed change, and falsehood, you
Can have no way but falsehood to be true?
Vain lunatic, against these 'scapes I could
                Dispute, and conquer, if I would,
                Which I abstain to do,
For by tomorrow, I may think so too.

The Flea

Mark but this flea, and mark in this,
How little that which thou deny'st me is;
Me it sucked first, and now sucks thee,
And in this flea, our two bloods mingled be;
Confess it, this cannot be said
A sin, or shame, or loss of maidenhead,
    Yet this enjoys before it woo,
     And pampered swells with one blood made of two,
     And this, alas, is more than we would do.

Oh stay, three lives in one flea spare,
Where we almost, nay more than married are.
This flea is you and I, and this
Our marriage bed, and marriage temple is;
Though parents grudge, and you, we'are met,
And cloistered in these living walls of jet.
    Though use make you apt to kill me,
    Let not to this, self murder added be,
    And sacrilege, three sins in killing three.

Cruel and sudden, hast thou since
Purpled thy nail, in blood of innocence?
In what could this flea guilty be,
Except in that drop which it sucked from thee?
Yet thou triumph'st, and say'st that thou
Find'st not thyself, nor me the weaker now;
    'Tis true, then learn how false, fears be;
    Just so much honour, when thou yield'st to me,
    Will waste, as this flea's death took life from thee.

Twicknam Garden

Blasted with sighs, and surrounded with tears,
　　Hither I come to seek the spring,
　　And at mine eyes, and at mine ears,
Receive such balms. as else cure everything;
　　But O, self traitor, I do bring
The spider love, which transubstantiates all,
　　And can convert manna to gall,
And that this place may thoroughly be thought
　　True paradise, I have the serpent brought.

'Twere wholesomer for me, that winter did
　　Benight the glory of this place,
　　And that a grave frost did forbid
These trees to laugh, and mock me to my face;
　　But that I may not this disgrace
Endure, nor yet leave loving, Love, let me
　　Some senseless piece of this place be;
Make me a mandrake, so I may groan here,
　　Or a stone fountain weeping out my year.

Hither with crystal vials, lovers come,
　　And take my tears, which are love's wine,
And try your mistress' tears at home,
For all are false, that taste not just like mine;
　　Alas, hearts do not in eyes shine,
Nor can you more judge woman's thoughts by tears,
　　Than by her shadow, what she wears.
O perverse sex, where none is true but she,
　　Who's therefore true, because her truth kills me.

Love's Alchemy

Some that have deeper digged love's mine than I,
Say, where his centric happiness doth lie:
      I have loved, and got, and told,
But should I love, get, tell, till I were old,
I should not find that hidden mystery;
      Oh, 'tis imposture all:
And as no chemic yet the elixir got,
      But glorifies his pregnant pot,
      If by the way to him befall
Some odoriferous thing, or medicinal,
  So, lovers dream a rich and long delight,
  But get a winter-seeming summer's night.

Our ease, our thrift, our honour, and our day,
Shall we, for this vain bubble's shadow pay?
      Ends love in this, that my man,
Can be as happy as I can; if he can
Endure the short scorn of a bridegroom's play?
      That loving wretch that swears,
'Tis not the bodies marry, but the minds,
      Which he in her angelic finds,
      Would swear as justly, that he hears,
In that day's rude hoarse minstrelsy, the spheres.
Hope not for mind in women; at their best
  Sweetness and wit, they are but mummy,
      possessed.

A Valediction: forbidding Mourning

As virtuous men pass mildly away,
   And whisper to their souls, to go,
Whilst some of their sad friends do say,
   The breath goes now, and some say, no:

So let us melt, and make no noise,
   No tear-floods, nor sigh-tempests move,
'Twere profanation of our joys
   To tell the laity our love.

Moving of th' earth brings harms and fears,
   Men reckon what it did and meant,
But trepidation of the spheres,
   Though greater far, is innocent.

Dull sublunary lovers' love
   (Whose soul is sense) cannot admit
Absence, because it doth remove
   Those things which elemented it.

But we by a love, so much refined,
   That our selves know not what it is,
Inter-assured of the mind,
   Care less, eyes, lips, and hands to miss.

Our two souls therefore, which are one,
 Though I must go, endure not yet
A breach, but an expansion,
 Like gold to aery thinness beat.

If they be two, they are two so
 As stiff twin compasses are two,
Thy soul the fixed foot, makes no show
 To move, but doth, if th'other do.

And though it in the centre sit,
 Yet when the other far doth roam,
It leans, and hearkens after it,
 And grows erect, as that comes home.

Such wilt thou be to me, who must
 Like th' other foot, obliquely run;
Thy firmness makes my circle just,
 And makes me end, where I begun.

The Relic

When my grave is broke up again
Some second guest to entertain,
(For graves have learned that woman-head
To be to more than one a bed)
        And he that digs it, spies
A bracelet of bright hair about the bone,
        Will he not let us alone,
And think that there a loving couple lies,
Who thought that this device might be some way
To make their souls, at the last busy day,
Meet at this grave, and make a little stay?

If this fall in a time, or land,
Where mis-devotion doth command,
Then, he that digs us up, will bring
Us, to the Bishop, and the King,
        To make us relics; then
Thou shalt be a Mary Magdalen, and I
        A something else thereby;
All women shall adore us, and some men;

And since at such time, miracles are sought,
I would have that age by this paper taught
What miracles we harmless lovers wrought.

      First, we loved well and faithfully,
      Yet knew not what we loved, nor why,
      Difference of sex no more we knew,
      Than our guardian angels do;
           Coming and going, we
Perchance might kiss, but not between those meals;
           Our hands ne'er touched the seals,
Which nature, injured by late law, sets free:
These miracles we did; but now alas,
All measure, and all language, I should pass,
Should I tell what a miracle she was.

A Nocturnal upon S. Lucy's Day,
being the shortest day

'Tis the year's midnight, and it is the day's,
Lucy's, who scarce seven hours herself unmasks,
   The sun is spent, and now his flasks
   Send forth light squibs, no constant rays;
     The world's whole sap is sunk:
The general balm th' hydroptic earth hath drunk,
Whither, as to the bed's-feet, life is shrunk,
Dead and interred; yet all these seem to laugh,
Compared with me, who am their epitaph.

Study me then, you who shall lovers be
At the next world, that is, at the next spring:
   For I am every dead thing,
   In whom love wrought new alchemy.
     For his art did express
A quintessence even from nothingness,
From dull privations, and lean emptiness
He ruined me, and I am re-begot
Of absence, darkness, death; things which are not.

All others, from all things, draw all that's good,
Life, soul, form, spirit, whence they being have;
   I, by love's limbeck, am the grave
   Of all, that's nothing. Oft a flood
     Have we two wept, and so
Drowned the whole world, us two; oft did we grow
To be two chaoses, when we did show
Care to aught else; and often absences
Withdrew our souls, and made us carcases.

But I am by her death (which word wrongs her)
Of the first nothing, the elixir grown;
    Were I a man, that I were one,
    I needs must know; I should prefer,
        If I were any beast,
Some ends, some means; yea plants, yea stones detest,
And love; all, all some properties invest;
If I an ordinary nothing were,
As shadow, a light, and body must be here.

But I am none; nor will my sun renew.
You lovers, for whose sake, the lesser sun
    At this time to the Goat is run
    To fetch new lust, and give it you,
        Enjoy your summer all;
Since she enjoys her long night's festival,
Let me prepare towards her, and let me call
This hour her vigil, and her eve, since this
Both the year's, and the day's deep midnight is.

Lines from 'Upon Mr Thomas Coryat's Crudities'

Oh to what height will love of greatness drive
Thy leavened spirit, sesqui-superlative?
Venice' vast lake thou hadst seen, and wouldst seek then
Some vaster thing, and found'st a courtesan.
That inland sea having discovered well,
A cellar gulf, where one might sail to hell
From Heidelberg, thou longed'st to see; and thou
This book, greater than all, producest now.
Infinite work, which doth so far extend,
That none can study it to any end.
'Tis no one thing, it is not fruit nor root;
Nor poorly limited with head or foot.
If man be therefore man, because he can
Reason, and laugh, thy book doth half make man.
One half being made, thy modesty was such,
That thou on th' other half wouldst never touch.
When wilt thou be at full, great lunatic?
Not till thou exceed the world? Canst thou be like
A prosperous nose-born wen, which sometimes grows
To be far greater than the mother-nose?

Elegy: Change

Although thy hand and faith, and good works too,
Have sealed thy love which nothing should undo,
Yea though thou fall back, that apostasy
Confirm thy love; yet much, much I fear thee.
Women are like the arts, forced unto none,
Open to all searchers, unprized, if unknown.
If I have caught a bird, and let him fly,
Another fowler using these means, as I,
May catch the same bird; and, as these things be,
Women are made for men, not him, nor me.
Foxes and goats, all beasts change when they please,
Shall women, more hot, wily, wild than these,
Be bound to one man, and did Nature then
Idly make them apter to endure than men?
They are our clogs, and their own; if a man be
Chained to a galley, yet the galley is free;
Who hath a plough-land, casts all his seed corn there,
And yet allows his ground more corn should bear;
Though Danuby into the sea must flow,
The sea receives the Rhine, Volga, and Po.
By nature, which gave it, this liberty
Thou lov'st, but Oh! canst thou love it and me?
Likeness glues love: then if so thou do,
To make us like and love, must I change too?
More than thy hate, I hate it, rather let me
Allow her change, than change as oft as she,

And so not teach, but force my opinion
To love not any one, nor every one.
To live in one land, is captivity,
To run all countries, a wild roguery;
Waters stink soon, if in one place they bide,
And in the vast sea are worse putrefied:
But when they kiss one bank, and leaving this
Never look back, but the next bank do kiss,
Then are they purest; change is the nursery
Of music, joy, life and eternity.

Elegy

Nature's lay idiot, I taught thee to love,
And in that sophistry, oh, thou dost prove
Too subtle: Fool, thou didst not understand
The mystic language of the eye nor hand:
Nor couldst thou judge the difference of the air
Of sighs, and say, this lies, this sounds despair:
Nor by th' eye's water call a malady
Desperately hot, or changing feverously.

I had not taught thee then, the alphabet
Of flowers, how they devisefully being set
And bound up, might with speechless secrecy
Deliver errands mutely, and mutually.
Remember since all thy words used to be
To every suitor, Ay, *if my friends agree*;
Since, household charms, thy husband's name to
    teach,
Were all the love-tricks, that thy wit could reach;
And since, an hour's discourse could scarce have
    made
One answer in thee, and that ill arrayed
In broken proverbs, and torn sentences.
Thou art not by so many duties his,
That from the world's common having severed
    thee,
Inlaid thee, neither to be seen, nor see,
As mine: who have with amorous delicacies
Refined thee into a blissful paradise.
Thy graces and good words my creatures be;
I planted knowledge and life's tree in thee,
Which oh, shall strangers taste? Must I alas
Frame and enamel plate, and drink in glass?
Chafe wax for others' seals? break a colt's force
And leave him then, being made a ready horse?

Elegy: To his Mistress Going to Bed

Come, Madam, come, all rest my powers defy,
Until I labour, I in labour lie.
The foe oft-times having the foe in sight,
Is tired with standing though they never fight.
Off with that girdle, like heaven's zone glistering,
But a far fairer world encompassing.
Unpin that spangled breastplate which you wear,
That th' eyes of busy fools may be stopped there.
Unlace yourself, for that harmonious chime
Tells me from you, that now 'tis your bed time.
Off with that happy busk, which I envy,
That still can be, and still can stand so nigh.
Your gown going off, such beauteous state reveals,
As when from flowery meads th' hill's shadow steals.
Off with that wiry coronet and show
The hairy diadem which on you doth grow;
Now off with those shoes, and then safely tread
In this love's hallowed temple, this soft bed.
In such white robes heaven's angels used to be
Received by men; thou angel bring'st with thee
A heaven like Mahomet's paradise; and though
Ill spirits walk in white, we easily know
By this these angels from an evil sprite,
Those set our hairs, but these our flesh upright.

Licence my roving hands, and let them go
Before, behind, between, above, below.
O my America, my new found land,
My kingdom, safeliest when with one man manned,
My mine of precious stones, my empery,
How blessed am I in this discovering thee!
To enter in these bonds, is to be free;
Then where my hand is set, my seal shall be.
    Full nakedness, all joys are due to thee.
As souls unbodied, bodies unclothed must be,
To taste whole joys. Gems which you women use
Are like Atlanta's balls, cast in men's views,
That when a fool's eye lighteth on a gem,
His earthly soul may covet theirs, not them.
Like pictures, or like books' gay coverings made
For laymen, are all women thus arrayed;
Themselves are mystic books, which only we
Whom their imputed grace will dignify
Must see revealed. Then since I may know,
As liberally, as to a midwife, show
Thyself: cast all, yea, this white linen hence,
Here is no penance, much less innocence.
    To teach thee, I am naked first, why then
What needst thou have more covering than a man.

Elegy: The Perfume

Once, and but once found in thy company,
All thy supposed escapes are laid on me;
And as a thief at bar, is questioned there
By all the men, that have been robbed that year,
So am I, (by this traitorous means surprised)
By thy hydroptic father catechized.
Though he had wont to search with glazed eyes,
As though he came to kill a cockatrice,
Though he have oft sworn, that he would remove
Thy beauty's beauty, and food of our love,
Hope of his goods, if I with thee were seen,
Yet close and secret, as our souls, we have been.
Though thy immortal mother which doth lie
Still buried in her bed, yet will not die,
Takes this advantage to sleep out day-light,
And watch thy entries, and returns all night,
And, when she takes thy hand, and would seem kind,
Doth search what rings, and armlets she can find,
And kissing notes the colour of thy face,
And fearing lest thou art swoll'n, doth thee embrace;
To try if thou long, doth name strange meats,
And notes thy paleness, blushing, sighs, and sweats;
And politicly will to thee confess
The sins of her own youth's rank lustiness;
Yet love these sorceries did remove, and move
Thee to gull thine own mother for my love.

Thy little brethren, which like faery sprites
Oft skipped into our chamber, those sweet nights,
And kissed, and ingled on thy father's knee,
Were bribed next day, to tell what they did see:
The grim eight-foot-high iron-bound serving-man,
That oft names God in oaths, and only then,
He that to bar the first gate, doth as wide
As the great Rhodian Colossus stride,
Which, if in hell no other pains there were,
Makes me fear hell, because he must be there:
Though by thy father he were hired to this,
Could never witness any touch or kiss.
But Oh, too common ill, I brought with me
That, which betrayed me to mine enemy:
A loud perfume, which at my entrance cried
Even at thy father's nose, so we were spied.
When, like a tyrant king, that in his bed
Smelt gunpowder, the pale wretch shivered.
Had it been some bad smell, he would have thought
That his own feet, or breath, that smell had wrought.
But as we in our isle imprisoned,
Where cattle only, and diverse dogs are bred,
The precious unicorns, strange monsters call,
So thought he good, strange, that had none at all.
I taught my silks, their whistling to forbear,
Even my oppressed shoes, dumb and speechless were,

Only, thou bitter sweet, whom I had laid
Next me, me traitorously hast betrayed,
And unsuspected hast invisibly
At once fled unto him, and stayed with me.
Base excrement of earth, which dost confound
Sense, from distinguishing the sick from sound;
By thee the silly amorous sucks his death
By drawing in a leprous harlot's breath;
By thee, the greatest stain to man's estate
Falls on us, to be called effeminate;
Though you be much loved in the prince's hall,
There, things that seem, exceed substantial.
Gods, when ye fumed on altars, were pleased well,
Because you were burnt, not that they liked your smell;
You are loathsome all, being taken simply alone,
Shall we love ill things joined, and hate each one?
If you were good, your good doth soon decay;
And you are rare, that takes the good away.
All my perfumes, I give most willingly
To embalm thy father's corse; What? will he die?

Hæc scribebat Marcús Sechlerús Augústanús
optimo ac generoso adolescenti Sebastiano
Fabio Augústano condiscipúlo súo longè ca
rissimo. A. D. 2 Cal: Martij A. 87.

HOLY SONNETS

Oh my black soul! now thou art summoned
By sickness, death's herald, and champion;
Thou art like a pilgrim, which abroad hath done
Treason, and durst not turn to whence he is fled,
Or like a thief, which till death's doom be read,
Wisheth himself delivered from prison;
But damned and haled to execution,
Wisheth that still he might be imprisoned;
Yet grace, if thou repent, thou canst not lack;
But who shall give thee that grace to begin?
Oh make thyself with holy mourning black,
And red with blushing, as thou art with sin;
Or wash thee in Christ's blood, which hath this might
That being red, it dyes red souls to white.

Death be not proud, though some have called thee
Mighty and dreadful, for, thou art not so,
For, those, whom thou think'st, thou dost overthrow,
Die not, poor death, nor yet canst thou kill me;
From rest and sleep, which but thy pictures be,
Much pleasure, then from thee, much more must flow,
And soonest our best men with thee do go,
Rest of their bones, and soul's delivery.
Thou art slave to fate, chance, kings, and desperate men,
And dost with poison, war, and sickness dwell,
And poppy, or charms can make us sleep as well,
And better than thy stroke; why swell'st thou then?
One short sleep past, we wake eternally,
And death shall be no more, Death thou shalt die.

At the round earth's imagined corners, blow
Your trumpets, angels, and arise, arise
From death, you numberless infinities
Of souls, and to your scattered bodies go,
All whom the flood did, and fire shall o'erthrow,
All whom war, dearth, age, agues, tyrannies,
Despair, law, chance hath slain, and you whose eyes,
Shall behold God, and never taste death's woe.
But let them sleep, Lord, and me mourn a space,
For, if above all these, my sins abound,
'Tis late to ask abundance of thy grace,
When we are there; here on this lowly ground,
Teach me how to repent; for that's as good
As if thou hadst sealed my pardon, with thy blood.

What if this present were the world's last night?
Mark in my heart, O soul, where thou dost dwell,
The picture of Christ crucified, and tell
Whether that countenance can thee affright,
Tears in his eyes quench the amazing light,
Blood fills his frowns, which from his pierced head fell,
And can that tongue adjudge thee unto hell,
Which prayed forgiveness for his foes' fierce spite?
No, no; but as in my idolatry
I said to all my profane mistresses,
Beauty, of pity, foulness only is
A sign of rigour: so I say to thee,
To wicked spirits are horrid shapes assigned,
This beauteous form assures a piteous mind.

Batter my heart, three-personed God; for, you
As yet but knock, breathe, shine, and seek to mend;
That I may rise, and stand, o'erthrow me, and bend
Your force, to break, blow, burn, and make me new.
I, like an usurped town, to another due,
Labour to admit you, but oh, to no end,
Reason your viceroy in me, me should defend,
But is captived, and proves weak or untrue,
Yet dearly'I love you, and would be loved fain,
But am betrothed unto your enemy,
Divorce me, untie, or break that knot again,
Take me to you, imprison me, for I
Except you enthral me, never shall be free,
Nor ever chaste, except you ravish me.

Oh, to vex me, contraries meet in one:
Inconstancy unnaturally hath begot
A constant habit; that when I would not
I change in vows, and in devotion.
As humorous is my contrition
As my profane love, and as soon forgot:
As riddlingly distempered, cold and hot,
As praying, as mute; as infinite, as none.
I durst not view heaven yesterday; and today
In prayers, and flattering speeches I court God:
Tomorow I quake with true fear of his rod.
So my devout fits come and go away
Like a fantastic ague: save that here
Those are my best days, when I shake with fear.

Since she whom I loved hath paid her last debt
To nature, and to hers, and my good is dead,
And her soul early into heaven ravished,
Wholly in heavenly things my mind is set.
Here the admiring her my mind did whet
To seek thee God; so streams do show the head,
But though I have found thee, and thou my thirst
    hast fed,
A holy thirsty dropsy melts me yet.
But why should I beg more love, when as thou
Dost woo my soul for hers; offering all thine:
And dost not only fear lest I allow
My love to saints and angels, things divine,
But in thy tender jealousy dost doubt
Lest the world, flesh, yea Devil put thee out.

Hymn to God my God, in my Sickness

Since I am coming to that holy room,
    Where, with thy choir of saints for evermore,
I shall be made thy music; as I come
    I tune the instrument here at the door,
    And what I must do then, think here before.

Whilst my physicians by their love are grown
    Cosmographers, and I their map, who lie
Flat on this bed, that by them may be shown
    That this is my south-west discovery
    Per fretum febris, by these straits to die,

I joy, that in these straits, I see my west;
    For, though their currents yield return to none,
What shall my west hurt me? As west and east
    In all flat maps (and I am one) are one,
    So death doth touch the resurrection.

Is the Pacific Sea my home? Or are
    The eastern riches? Is Jerusalem?
Anyan, and Magellan, and Gibraltar,
    All straits, and none but straits, are ways to them,
    Whether where Japhet dwelt, or Cham, or Shem.

We think that Paradise and Calvary,
    Christ's Cross, and Adam's tree, stood in one place;
Look Lord, and find both Adams met in me;
    As the first Adam's sweat surrounds my face,
    May the last Adam's blood my soul embrace.

So, in his purple wrapped receive me Lord,
    By these his thorns give me his other crown;
And as to others' souls I preached thy word,
    Be this my text, my sermon to mine own,
    Therefore that he may raise the Lord throws down.

NOTES ON THE PICTURES

p.6 *Portrait of John Donne*, early seventeenth century, artist unknown. In the collection of The Marquis of Lothian.

p.15 *Venetia Stanley, Lady Digby*, c.1615-17, miniature by Peter Oliver. Reproduced by courtesy of the Board of Trustees of the Victoria and Albert Museum, London.

p.19 *A Man and his Wife*, c. 1540s, Italian School. Reproduced by courtesy of the Trustees, The National Gallery, London.

p.22 *A Man Clutching a Hand in the Clouds*, 1588, miniature by Nicholas Hilliard. Reproduced by courtesy of the Board of Trustees of the Victoria and Albert Museum, London.

p.27 *Henry Percy, 9th Earl of Northumberland*, c.1595, by Nicholas Hilliard. The Rijksmuseum, Amsterdam.

p.30 *A Mathematician*, 1600-50, Emilian School. Reproduced by courtesy of the Trustees, The National Gallery, London.

p.35 *Lucy Harrington, Countess of Bedford, in Masque Costume*, 1606, attributed to John De Critz. Reproduced by kind permission of The Marquess of Tavistock and the Trustees of the Bedford Estates, Woburn Abbey.

p.39 *Lady Elizabeth Pope*, c.1615-20, attributed to Robert Peake the Elder. The Tate Gallery, London.

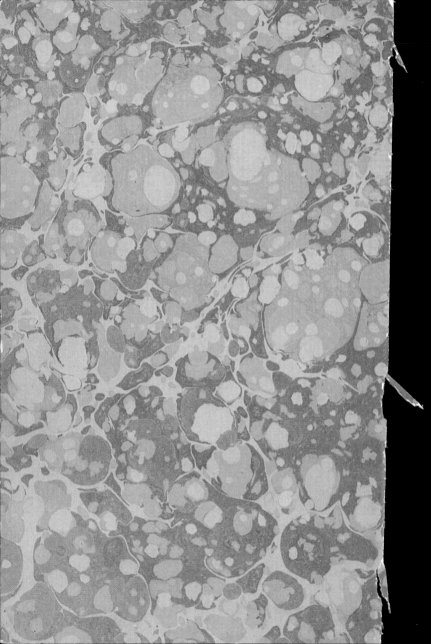